Bob Chilcott
Jussi Chydenius

Sun, Moon, Sea, and Stars

8 contemporary pieces for mixed voices

MUSIC DEPARTMENT

OXFORD
UNIVERSITY PRESS

OXFORD
UNIVERSITY PRESS

Great Clarendon Street, Oxford OX2 6DP,
United Kingdom

Oxford University Press is a department of the University of Oxford.
It furthers the University's aim of excellence in research, scholarship,
and education by publishing worldwide

Oxford is a registered trade mark of Oxford University Press
in the UK and in certain other countries

Impression: 1

ISBN 978-0-19-338814-7

Music origination by
Enigma Music Production Services, Amersham, Bucks.

Printed in Great Britain on acid-free paper by
Halstan & Co. Ltd, Amersham, Bucks.

Preface

We are both lucky to have sung in world-class vocal groups: The King's Singers and Rajaton. When you have sung in groups such as these—made up of six voices—the sound of interlocking vocal textures and richly coloured harmony never leaves you. Both of us have been strongly influenced by the vocal group 'sound', and we have inevitably incorporated a great deal of the rhythmic impulse and harmonic language of small-group singing into our pieces.

In this book we have tried to capture a bit of this feeling in eight new songs, designed to be sung either by a small group or by a choir. Our hope is that these songs, with opportunities for improvisation and jazz combo or band accompaniment, are flexible enough to allow groups to personalize them, while incorporating into their repertoire a little of the style and sound that has been so important to us.

BOB CHILCOTT AND JUSSI CHYDENIUS
January 2013

Contents

Composers' Notes   5

Come back!   Bob Chilcott   6

Tonight   Jussi Chydenius   12

My Heart's Friend   Bob Chilcott   22

Deep in the night   Jussi Chydenius   30

Sun, Moon, Sea, and Stars   Bob Chilcott   41

On a Windy Day   Jussi Chydenius   52

She walks in beauty   Bob Chilcott   60

The Sound of the Sea   Jussi Chydenius   71

Composers' Notes

I have set a great deal of Native American poetry over the years, and **My Heart's Friend** is one of the most well known and personal of these. I stole the piano introduction from an arrangement of a Jimmy Webb song that I made for The King's Singers and Richard Rodney Bennett a number of years ago, and I tried to incorporate the feeling of a Jimmy Webb song into the melody line. **Come back!** sets my own words, but the inspiration came from a Seminole poem entitled 'Song for the Dying'.

I have always been a great admirer of the French musician Michel Legrand, and I particularly love his 'Once upon a summertime', to lyrics by Johnny Mercer. I tried to reflect his bittersweet style in **Sun, Moon, Sea, and Stars**, and I imagined it sung by The King's Singers. I have given a contemporary twist to the Lord Byron poem **She walks in beauty**, which includes the opportunity for a bit of vocal improvisation, and as with a few of the pieces in this collection, the accompaniment is flexible.

I have never been a musical purist, and I hope that these songs will give the opportunity for the singers to use their creativity and stylistic flair.

BOB CHILCOTT

I am a hopeless romantic and an utterly text-oriented composer. For me, composing without a touching poem is like riding a bicycle with a flat tyre—you move forward, but it's slow and certainly not fun.

On a Windy Day was the first piece I wrote for this collection, and it sets a beautiful poem by Anne Brontë. I wanted to keep the piano accompaniment simple, to match the style of the ballad, which should be performed with a wide dynamic range. **Tonight** is a love song that sounds to me as if it could appear in a French film—very romantic but a bit melancholic. Choirs should feel free to alter the scat syllables in my *a cappella* pieces. If you would rather use 'bm' than 'dm' or 'doo' than 'oo', then do it!

I was haunted by the poem **Deep in the night** by Sara Teasdale, and I felt it needed to be set to music. The downward chromatic melody in the tenors is the harmonic key to this piece, but the emphasis should be on the text and the tightness of the rhythms—make it funky but poetic. **The Sound of the Sea** is the 'biggest' of my four pieces, with piano and optional bass and drums accompaniment, and the opportunity for choirs to exploit their full dynamic range.

JUSSI CHYDENIUS

for David Lawrence and CBSO Young Voices

Come back!

Words and music by
BOB CHILCOTT
(b. 1955)

**Bars 1–4 (and all repetitions) should be played as written. Elsewhere, the piano part may be performed *ad lib.* An optional bass and drum kit part is available in PDF form as a free download from the publisher's website.

Tonight

Sara Teasdale
(1884–1933)

JUSSI CHYDENIUS
(b. 1972)

22

for Tim and Natalie

My Heart's Friend

Mary Austin (abridged)
(1868–1934)

BOB CHILCOTT
(b. 1955)

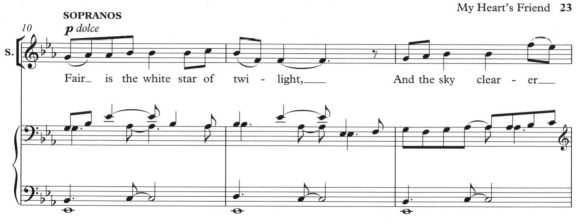

SOPRANOS
p dolce

Fair_ is the white star of twi - light,_____ And the sky clear - er_____

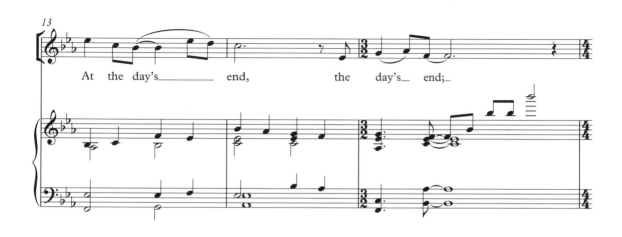

At the day's_____ end, the day's_ end;_

mp dolce

She is fair-er, she is dear - er,_____ She,_____ my

She is fair-er, she is dear - er, She,_____ my

She is fair-er, bet-ter worth lov - ing,_____ She,_____ my

She is fair-er, bet-ter worth lov - ing, She,_____ my

heart's_ friend. She is fair-er, bet-ter worth lov - ing,_____

heart's, my heart's_ friend. She is fair-er, bet-ter worth lov - ing,

She,_____ my heart's_ friend. She is fair-er, bet-ter worth

She,_____ my heart's, my heart's_ friend. She is fair-er,

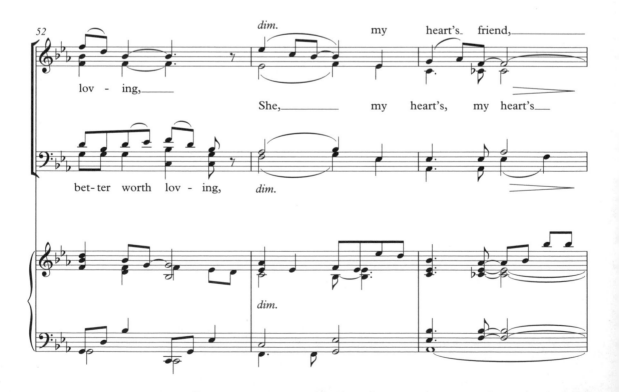

lov - ing,_____ my heart's_ friend,_____

She,_____ my heart's, my heart's__

bet- ter worth lov - ing, *dim.*

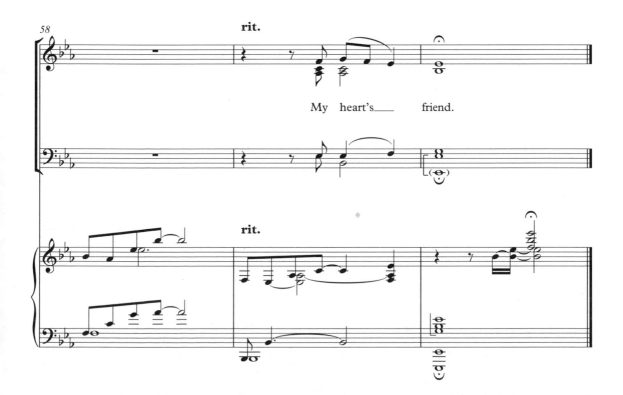

Deep in the night

Sara Teasdale
(1884–1933)

JUSSI CHYDENIUS
(b. 1972)

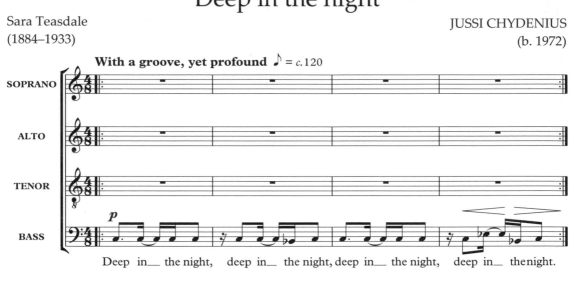

cry__ for - ev - er lost as the swal - low's flight,__ seek-

deep in__ the night, deep in__ the night, deep in__ the night,

- ing for you__ and__ ne - ver, ne - ver stilled by the stars__ at

deep in__ the night, deep in__ the night.

oo_____

night._____

oo_____

Deep in__ the night, deep in__ the night, deep in__ the night, deep in__ the night,

*Keyboard reduction for rehearsal only.

o - ver the world   to   you.   Love in my heart   is   a

o - ver the world   to   you.   Love in my heart   is   a

deep   in___ the night,   deep in___ the night, deep   in___ the night,

cry___ for - ev - er   lost as the swal - low's   flight,___   seek-

cry   for - ev - er   lost as the swal - low's   flight,___   seek-

deep   in___ the night, deep   in___ the night,   deep in___ the night,

- ing for you___ and___ ne - ver, ne - ver stilled by the stars___ at

- ing for you___ and ne - ver, ne - ver stilled by the stars___ at

deep in___ the night, deep in___ the night.

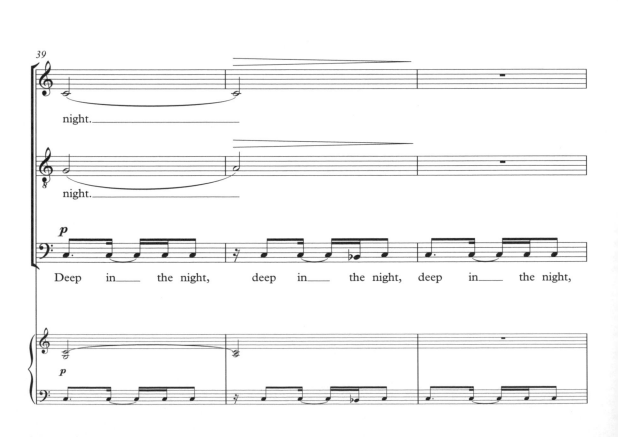

night._____

night._____

p

Deep in___ the night, deep in___ the night, deep in___ the night,

p

for Kate

Sun, Moon, Sea, and Stars

Words and music by
BOB CHILCOTT
(b. 1955)

*The keyboard reduction does not include the solo baritone part.   †Alternatively, this part may be sung by Bass 1.

hold it in___ our hand.   You and I___ will pierce the sky___ like

oo___

oo___

oo___

rain - drops in   the sand.   And   when the sun - light shows its face it's

when   the   sun -   light

when   the   sun -   light

sun   -   -   light

You and I___ will catch a star___ and cra - dle it___ with love.___

poco rit.

40

sun, moon, sea, and stars___ to me.___

sun, moon, stars.

___ stars.___ oo___ And

sun, stars.

___ stars.___ oo___ And

sun, stars. oo___ And

42 **a little slower and freer**

p

You're

with the star - light look - ing down it's on - ly plain_ to see,___

with the star - light look - ing down it's on - ly plain_ to see,___

with the star - light look - ing down it's on - ly plain_ to see,___

a little slower and freer

On a Windy Day

Anne Brontë
(1820–49)

JUSSI CHYDENIUS
(b. 1972)

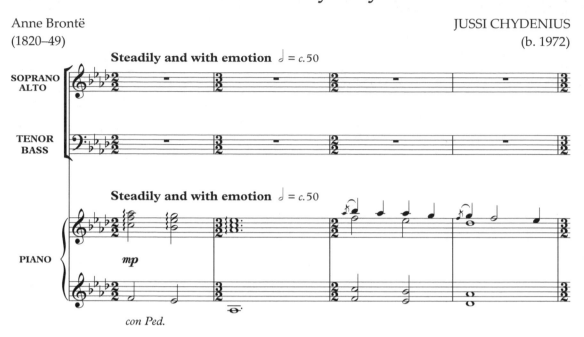

An optional bass and drum kit part is available in PDF form as a free download from the publisher's website.

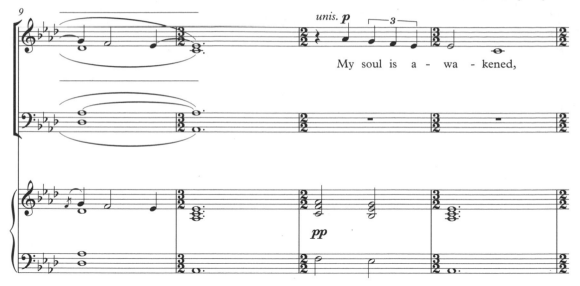

My soul is a - wa - kened,

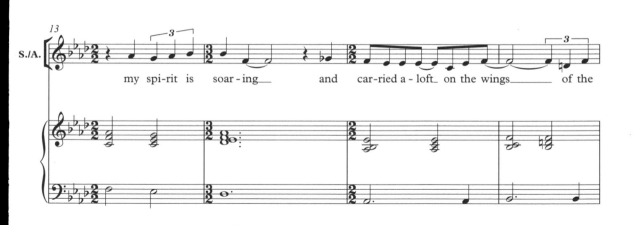

S./A.

my spi-rit is soar-ing___ and car-ried a-loft_ on the wings_____ of the

breeze,_____ and car-ried a-loft_ on the wings_ of the

the dead leaves be - neath them_____ are

mer - ri - ly danc - ing,_____ the white clouds are scud - ding a -

- cross the_____ blue sky, a - cross the blue sky.

SOPRANOS & ALTOS
unis. **p**

S./A.

I wish I could see how   the o-cean is lash-ing___   the

foam of its bil-lows to whirl - winds of spray,_____ the

foam of its bil-lows to whirl - winds of spray;

I wish I could see how its proud waves are

unis.

Ped._____

for Bruce Rogers and Mt. San Antonio College Singcopation

She walks in beauty

Lord Byron
(1788–1824)

BOB CHILCOTT
(b. 1955)

*The piano part may be performed *ad lib*. An optional bass and drum kit part is available in PDF form as a free download from the publisher's website.

The smiles that win, the tints that glow, But tell of days in good-ness spent,_____ A mind at peace with

*This repeat can be taken any number of times, at the performers' discretion. The vocal lines can be embellished *ad lib.* or sung as written.

†Diminuendo last time only.

The Sound of the Sea

Henry Wadsworth Longfellow
(1807–82)

JUSSI CHYDENIUS
(b. 1972)

An optional bass and drum kit part is available in PDF form as a free download from the publisher's website.